MY DADDY LONGLEGS

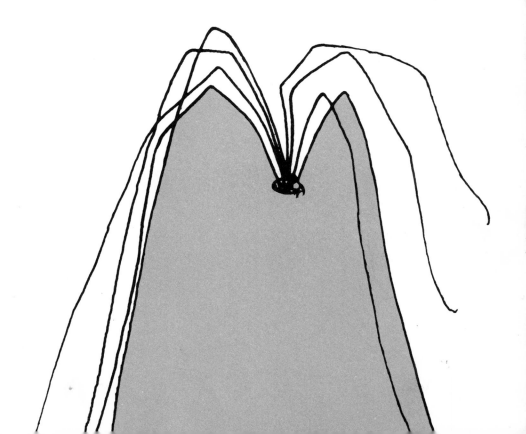

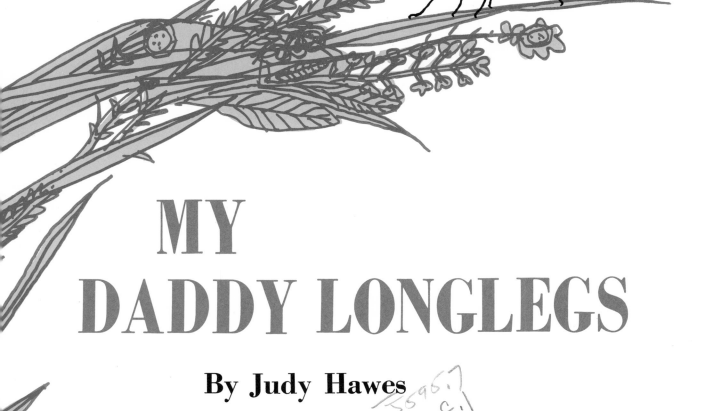

MY
DADDY LONGLEGS

By Judy Hawes

Illustrated by Walter Lorraine

Thomas Y. Crowell Company   New York

LET'S-READ-AND-FIND-OUT SCIENCE BOOKS

Editors: *DR. ROMA GANS*, Professor Emeritus of Childhood Education, Teachers College, Columbia University

DR. FRANKLYN M. BRANLEY, Chairman and Astronomer of The American Museum–Hayden Planetarium

Air Is All Around You
Animals in Winter
A Baby Starts to Grow
Bats in the Dark
Bees and Beelines
Before You Were a Baby
The Big Dipper
Big Tracks, Little Tracks
Birds at Night
Birds Eat and Eat and Eat
Bird Talk
The Blue Whale
The Bottom of the Sea
The Clean Brook
Cockroaches:
  Here, There, and Everywhere
Down Come the Leaves
A Drop of Blood
Ducks Don't Get Wet
The Emperor Penguins
Find Out by Touching
Fireflies in the Night
Flash, Crash, Rumble, and Roll
Floating and Sinking
Follow Your Nose
Fossils Tell of Long Ago
Giraffes at Home
Glaciers

Gravity Is a Mystery
Green Turtle Mysteries
Hear Your Heart
High Sounds, Low Sounds
Hot as an Ice Cube
How a Seed Grows
How Many Teeth?
How You Talk
Hummingbirds in the Garden
Icebergs
In the Night
It's Nesting Time
Ladybug, Ladybug, Fly
  Away Home
The Listening Walk
*Look at Your Eyes**
A Map Is a Picture
The Moon Seems to Change
Mushrooms and Molds
My Daddy Longlegs
My Five Senses
My Hands
My Visit to the Dinosaurs
North, South, East, and West
Oxygen Keeps You Alive
Rain and Hail
Rockets and Satellites

Salt
Sandpipers
Seeds by Wind and Water
Shrimps
The Skeleton Inside You
Snow Is Falling
Spider Silk
Starfish
*Straight Hair, Curly Hair**
The Sun: Our Nearest Star
The Sunlit Sea
A Tree Is a Plant
Upstairs and Downstairs
Use Your Brain
Watch Honeybees with Me
Water for Dinosaurs and You
Weight and Weightlessness
What Happens to a Hamburger
What I Like About Toads
What Makes a Shadow?
What Makes Day and Night
*What the Moon Is Like**
Where Does Your Garden Grow?
Where the Brook Begins
Why Frogs Are Wet
The Wonder of Stones
*Your Skin and Mine**

*AVAILABLE IN SPANISH

L.C. Card 74-175107   ISBN 0-690-56655-7   0-690-56656-5 (LB)

1   2   3   4   5   6   7   8   9   10

MY DADDY LONGLEGS

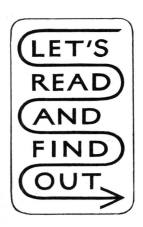

Can you hear with your legs? A daddy longlegs can. Can you smell or taste with your legs? A daddy longlegs can do that, too.

A daddy longlegs has eight long, thin legs. His legs are so long, a daddy longlegs seems to be standing on stilts. When he walks, his body bounces up and down between his legs. He looks as if he were dancing. Sometimes his body droops way below his knees.

A daddy longlegs can travel very fast. He doesn't have to crawl on the ground. He can skim along on top of the grass.

A daddy longlegs has four pairs of legs. The first pair is nearest the head. The second pair is much longer than any of the others. A daddy longlegs keeps waving his second pair of legs all about him. He touches everything he can reach. He uses these legs to touch, hear, taste, and smell.

Daddy longlegs spend much of their time cleaning or "preening" their long legs, especially their second legs. They clean a leg by pulling it slowly through their jaws. Then they wash their jaws in water. Only clean legs can do a good job of touching, tasting, smelling, and hearing.

To learn more about daddy longlegs, you should go out and catch some. Early fall is the best time. Look on dark, damp walls, outside cellar windows, or near rainspouts.

When you try to catch a daddy longlegs, be very careful. If you touch a leg, the daddy longlegs will drop to the ground and scamper away. If you grab a leg, the leg will come off. The lost leg will keep wriggling.

While you are watching this, the daddy longlegs runs away on seven legs. This is one way a daddy longlegs protects itself.

The poor daddy longlegs cannot grow a new leg. He will simply have to get along without it. I often see a daddy longlegs with only six or seven legs. But if a daddy longlegs loses both of his second legs, he is almost helpless. These are his most important legs.

Be very gentle so that your daddy longlegs doesn't lose a leg. Hold a glass over the whole daddy long-legs. Be careful to get all his legs inside the glass. Jiggle the glass a little to make the daddy long-legs crawl inside it. Put your hand over the glass so he won't get out.

Take the glass to a table and turn the glass over quickly. Look at the daddy longlegs with a magnifying glass. You will see four tiny black bumps along each side of the daddy longlegs' body. They're where the eight long legs are fastened to the body. Each leg has seven joints. The two "knees" are the easiest joints to see.

All of the legs are covered with short, stiff hairs. These hairs give the daddy longlegs his sense of touch.

On the second pair of legs, at each joint, there are also rows of very fine hairs. These hairs are the daddy longlegs' "ears." You can test his hearing. Make a loud noise near a daddy longlegs. His second pair of legs will jerk right away.

Do you see some dark patches at the tips of the second pair of legs? These are for smelling and tasting.

Each of the eight legs ends in a small claw. The daddy longlegs uses these claws to grab hold of blades of grass. They keep him from slipping as he runs along the top of the grass.

Near the small slit of a mouth, there are two feelers which look like a smaller pair of legs. There is also a pair of pincers or claws. When the second legs find food, the feelers push it into the pincers. The pincers crush the food. Then they put it into the mouth.

The small body of a daddy longlegs is round or oval and is marked into sections. It has no neck and no waist. On each side of the body the daddy longlegs has breathing holes. Some daddy longlegs have extra breathing holes in their legs. See if you can find them on your daddy longlegs.

A dot on the top of the body is really a tiny lookout tower. There is an eye on each side of the dot. The eyes stare sideways without blinking.

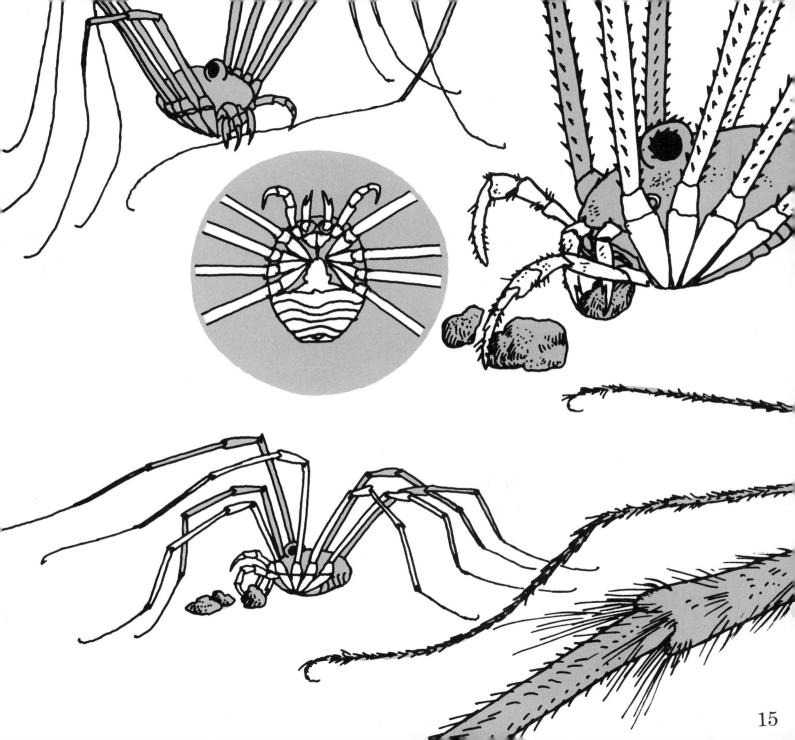

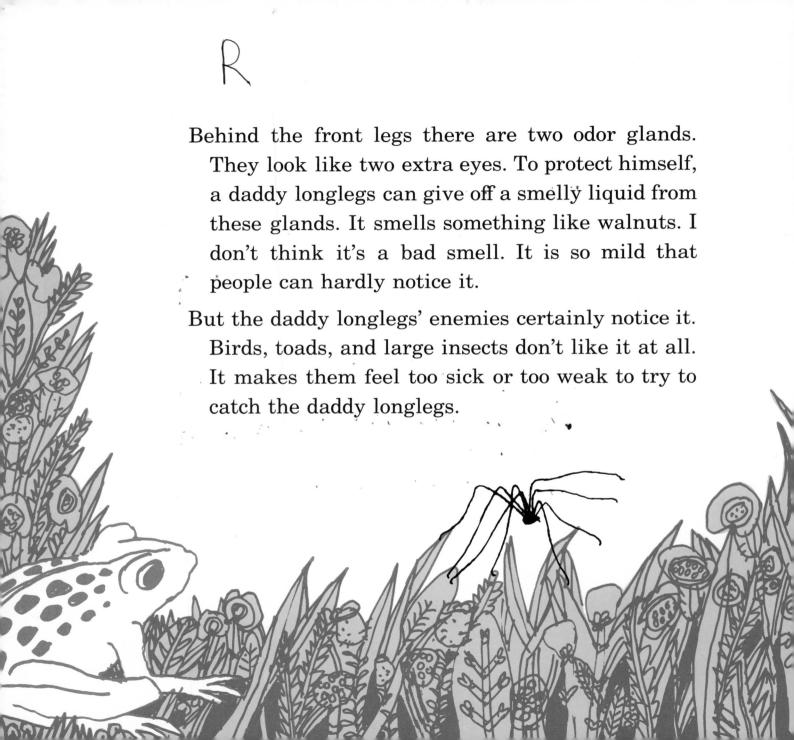

Behind the front legs there are two odor glands. They look like two extra eyes. To protect himself, a daddy longlegs can give off a smelly liquid from these glands. It smells something like walnuts. I don't think it's a bad smell. It is so mild that people can hardly notice it.

But the daddy longlegs' enemies certainly notice it. Birds, toads, and large insects don't like it at all. It makes them feel too sick or too weak to try to catch the daddy longlegs.

The dull coloring of the daddy longlegs is another way he is protected from his enemies. Daddy longlegs are awfully hard to see as they wobble along in the grass.

Daddy longlegs are related to spiders, but they are not true spiders. Daddy longlegs don't spin webs to trap insects for food the way spiders do. Daddy longlegs go out hunting for their food. Daddy longlegs never bite people, and they are never poisonous.

In late summer and early fall the daddy longlegs mate. Soon afterward the female daddy longlegs lays about twenty or thirty tiny pale green eggs. She lays them in damp sand, under stones, or behind tree bark. Most eggs are laid in the fall and do not hatch until spring. Adult daddy longlegs usually die late in the fall. A few may sleep through the winter.

When the babies hatch out of their shells, they look like their parents, but they are much, much smaller. They are tinier than a pinhead! But they grow quickly.

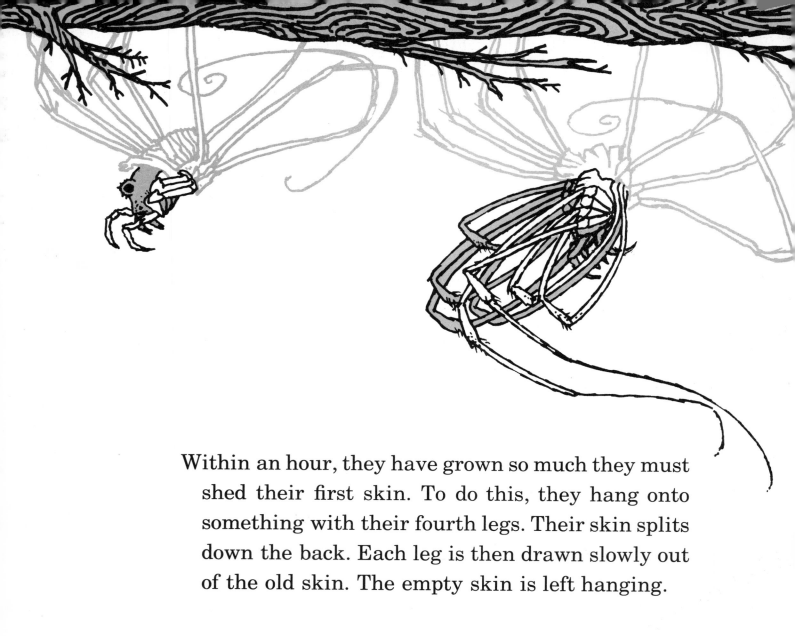

Within an hour, they have grown so much they must shed their first skin. To do this, they hang onto something with their fourth legs. Their skin splits down the back. Each leg is then drawn slowly out of the old skin. The empty skin is left hanging.

The young daddy longlegs shed their skin every ten
days. After they have done this five to nine times,
they are fully grown.

I made a cage for my daddy longlegs so I could watch them. It is a large cardboard box, but it isn't very deep. A few little holes in the sides give plenty of air. I covered the bottom with a piece of plastic and put damp sand on it. For shelter I added a few stones and twigs, and some dead leaves. I put a small dish filled with water in the cage, too. Then I covered the top with a piece of plastic.

Ten or twenty daddy longlegs live together in my cage. It is fun to watch them at night. They are more active then. They rest during the day.

If I look into my daddy longlegs' cage when they are resting, my shadow wakes them suddenly. Then they scamper around the cage, bouncing up and down in their funny dance. A few minutes later they are all resting quietly again.

what does in eat.

Feeding daddy longlegs is easy. They usually eat living insects, such as mites, spiders, caterpillars, and centipedes. If I can't find any of these, I give them bread crumbs, or butter, or other fat. They really seem to like lamb fat. They eat often, but never very much.

I keep the cage in a cool, shady place, so the sand won't dry out. Daddy longlegs need a lot of moisture. They are always thirsty. Their second legs help them find water.

Daddy longlegs can't swim, but they can stand on water. They often stand on top of the water to drink.

If direct sun ever shone on the cage, my daddy longlegs would curl up and die. They don't mind the cold, so long as it is damp. Some daddy longlegs have lived through subzero weather. Their legs were pulled up into one stiff bundle, as if they were dead. They became lively again when held in a man's warm hand for only a few seconds.

31

After you have watched your daddy longlegs for a few days, set them free outside. You can catch more any time you like.

ABOUT THE AUTHOR

In her research for MY DADDY LONGLEGS, Judy Hawes had the assistance of the children of Eagle Camp, in South Hero, Vermont, who eagerly helped her catch and observe the insects.

Mrs. Hawes, mother of four, has worked with children as a teacher and as a leader in scouting and Sunday school. For the past ten years she has taught various kinds of special education classes in the public schools. She is the author of eight books in the Let's-Read-and-Find-Out series, among them *Fireflies in the Night, Shrimps,* and *Why Frogs Are Wet.*

A native of Forest Hills, New York, Mrs. Hawes was graduated from Vassar College. She and her husband are residents of Glen Rock, New Jersey, where they participate in many community activities. They are both avid tennis players.

ABOUT THE ARTIST

Walter Lorraine has long been acknowledged as one of our country's leading illustrators and designers of books for children. More than thirty of his books have been chosen for Children's Book Shows of the American Institute of Graphic Arts, and two titles have been selected by *The New York Times* for its list of best-illustrated books.

Mr. Lorraine was born in Worcester, Massachusetts, and received a B.F.A. degree from the Rhode Island School of Design. He currently teaches graphic design at Northeastern University and has taught typography at Boston University, and book illustration and design at the Museum School of Fine Arts. With his wife and four children he lives in Newton, Massachusetts.